Three-dimensi
Découpage

Vivien Crook

SEARCH PRESS

First published in Great Britain 1996
Search Press Limited
Wellwood, North Farm Road,
Tunbridge Wells, Kent TN2 3DR

Reprinted 1996, 1997, 1998, 1999

The author and publishers would like to thank the following for their help in the production of this book:

Dorset Découpage, Corfe Mullen, Dorset, for the supply of the floral pictures by Sonie Ames that are used on the front cover and on pages 3 and 19;

Jan Michal Studios for the prints used on pages 16–17;

Robbert Snel of Uitgeverij Jorrit, Noordwijk aan zee, Holland, for permission to use the paintings by Anton Pieck which appear on pages 20–22, 24–27, 47 and the back cover;

Klein Kraft, Chesterfield, Derbyshire, for permission to use the print of strawberries on page 48;

Murray Marketing, Leicester, for the wrapping paper used to make the fruit picture on page 6;

Noel Tatt Group, Canterbury, Kent, for permission to use the prints from their range *Prints for Découpage* on pages 28–31;

Robin Sudbury & Associates, Altringham, Cheshire, for permission to use and for suppying prints of *The Cellist* by Paul Bennet on page 23, and for supplying various other prints;

Royal Society for the Protection of Birds for permission to use the wrapping papers and tags on pages 40–41;

John Arnold Publishing, Stoke-on-Trent, for permission to use the pictures of fuchsias by Rob Pohl on pages 18 and 47;

Personal Stamp Exchange, Petaluma, California, for the rubber stamps used for the pictures on pages 1 and 38–39.

ISBN 0 85532 808 8

Printed in Spain by Elkar S. Coop, Bilbao 48012

Summer fruit

Some of the leaves in this picture blended into the background, but with a little imagination I managed to raise them successfully.

Contents

A selection of the different types of subject that can be converted to three-dimensional images.

Introduction

I first became interested in three-dimensional découpage while serving on a jury. There happened to be a craft shop near the court, and one lunch hour I was tempted by the window display to buy two kits. I started to work on one of them that same evening and by the end of my two weeks' service I had finished both. Not only that, but I could not wait to do more – in fact, I was hooked.

I soon realised that I could get more enjoyment, and produce what I felt was a more satisfactory result, by breaking away from commercially produced kits and simply 'doing my own thing'. I have been doing just that for some six years now, and I still enjoy it.

The art of three-dimensional découpage lies in creating a lifelike picture that has physical depth as well as shape and colour. If it is a street scene, you feel as though you could walk into it; if it is a flower, you want to reach out and touch it. The effect is produced by taking several copies of the same picture, then cutting, shaping and building them up in layers so that the foreground of the picture is actually, as well as seemingly, separated from the background. This reinforces the illusion of depth created by the original artist.

It is a very enjoyable and relaxing art form. It is also extremely rewarding to be able to look at something which you have created yourself and which is therefore unique. On the other hand, it can be very addictive. You will find yourself looking at greetings cards, gift wrapping paper, commercially produced prints, in fact any sort of picture, in a new light and thinking, 'Now that would look good.'

The materials and tools required are not expensive, and in the following pages I show you the techniques and tips I have learned so that with time, care and patience you can create your own masterpieces.

History

The origins of three-dimensional découpage are rather obscure, but we do know that beautiful, exotic lacquered furniture began to arrive in Europe from China in the seventeenth century. An enterprising person then had the idea of reproducing the effect by simply gluing cut-out Chinese prints on to pieces of furniture and other household items and protecting them with a coat of varnish.

French cabinet-makers then improved on this basic method by using more delicate prints, such as flowers and cherubs, and coating them with many layers of varnish so that the pictures appeared to be inlaid. These craftsmen gave us the descriptive term découpage, which comes from the French verb *découper*, meaning 'to cut out'.

Naturally, these pictures were essentially flat; just how flat depended on the number of coats of varnish – some craftsmen used twenty or more layers. It is not known who conceived the idea of three-dimensional découpage, but it first became popular with the Victorians, who used slices of cork to separate the different elements, or layers, of the picture.

The popularity of this craft took on a new lease of life in the mid-eighties and, currently, it shows no sign of abating. Techniques are being improved all the time and there are now many companies who specialise in selling sets of prints that have been selected as being particularly suitable for three-dimensional treatment.

I found this lovely bunch of fruit on a sheet of gift wrap paper. The leaves were quite easy to shape but the fruit presented a little more difficulty because of their roundness. I used just my fingers and a lot of patience to ease the edges down smoothly.

Watercolour pictures are very difficult to convert to three-dimensional images. This landscape has good depth but it does not have clearly defined edges. The trees on either side could not be separated successfully from the sky, while the reflection in the water would look as though it was floating on top of the river. Also, there is nothing in the foreground that could be built up to provide a focal point.

The picture of a cellist is an example of a good subject for three-dimensional découpage. It has clearly defined edges and it has obvious layers. A three-dimensional version of this picture is shown on page 23.

Choosing your subject

When choosing a picture, look for one that has clearly defined edges to the various elements. Sharp outlines make cutting out so much easier.

The material on which the picture is printed is also important. It should not be too thick nor should it have a high-gloss surface finish – in both cases the material is likely to crack when you try to shape the pieces. Thick material also shows more white edge when it is cut and this will require more work to hide it (see page 12). On the other hand, if the paper is too thin it will crease too easily, which is equally frustrating.

Bearing these criteria in mind, virtually any subject is suitable for three-dimensional treatment. I would suggest you start by using specifically selected prints – a wide range is available from art and craft shops, and through mail-order outlets. You can then start to experiment with other source materials (see pages 8–9).

Flowers and plants are really striking subjects. Start with a small arrangement (one that has just a few flowers with simple shapes) and concentrate on getting the different layers of leaves and petals sorted out properly. As you gain confidence, start to shape the petals and progress to more complicated arrangements.

Simple figures readily take to being layered. You can use as much detailing as your skill will allow and still end up with a pleasing result.

Buildings and street scenes that have in-built perspective are also very good subjects. However, general landscapes have to be selected with care.

Very realistic effects on birds and animals can be obtained by using the 'feathering' technique which I shall describe later.

The scope for subjects is very wide, and I am sure that soon you will want to try to bring to life all sorts of pictures.

Materials

You will need a set of identical copies of your chosen picture – to start with, I suggest a minimum of six. If the scene is complicated, and you want to include lots of detail, use more. I always keep one copy as a reference while building a picture; this will come in handy if you make a mistake or if you suddenly spot extra details that you want to include. Decide how many copies you need and buy them all at one time. Recently, I went back to buy a couple of extra prints, only to find that the new ones were reproduced at a slightly different size from my original set!

Specialist prints (as individual copies or as packaged sets and kits) are available from some craft shops or by mail-order from specialist suppliers. These are the obvious choice for the beginner. However, you can achieve very good results with other types of source material.

Colour photocopies are readily available and you might be surprised at the quality of colour reproduction.

Photographs can be given the three-dimensional treatment, but you must be very selective when choosing your subject.

Colour photocopies

Specialist prints

Photographs

Rubber stamping is quite a popular craft in itself, but you can also give your pictures a three-dimensional finish.

Gift wrap, especially if it has a repeat image, is a good source for small designs. Some wrapping papers are rather flimsy and will need careful handling. Gift tags printed on lightweight card can also be made into three-dimensional images.

A simple drawing can be made into a beautiful three-dimensional picture using good-quality sheets of different coloured plain papers. This is an ideal method of introducing this craft to children.

If you intend to frame your work you will also need some backing board. This should be stiff enough not to bend when mounted in a frame but not too heavy in weight. I find that a thickness of between 1.5 and 3mm ($^1/_{16}$ and $^1/_8$in) is ideal. You can buy it in most art and craft shops; you could also try talking to your local picture framer – he may be willing to sell you some offcuts. Remember to size the backing board to the frame, which could be considerably larger than the picture.

Tools and techniques

Only a few tools are required to make a three-dimensional picture: a good pair of scissors, a craft knife, a steel-edged ruler, a cutting mat, a pair of tweezers, some cocktail sticks, a soft pencil and a soft brush. You will also need some silicone rubber adhesive and varnish.

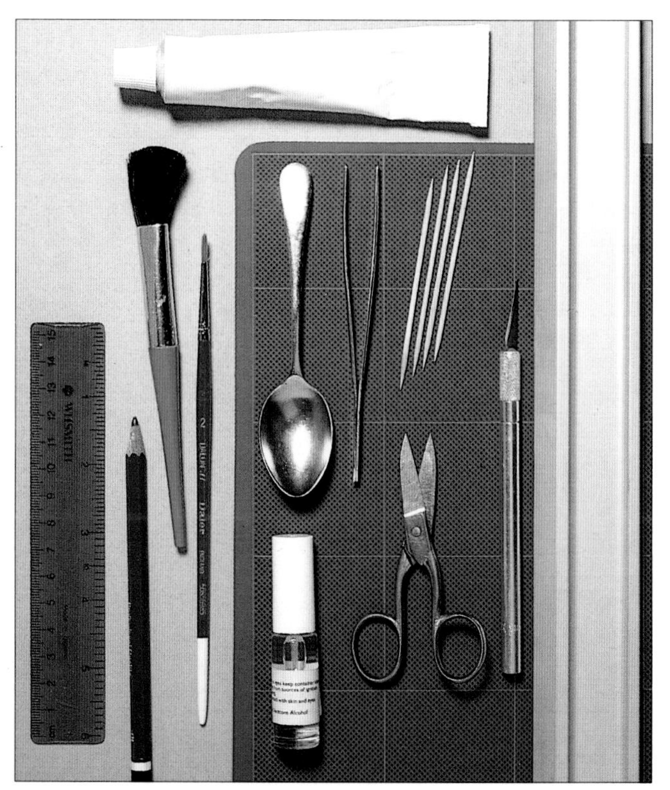

The tools for cutting, shaping and assembling a picture.

Cutting

Before you even start to think about picking up your scissors, take the time to study your picture thoroughly. Consider which parts of the picture are closest to you, which are furthest away and which are the most important. The number of copies that you have will limit the number of layers in the finished picture. This in turn will determine how much detail you can highlight and whether any detail must remain as part of the background layer.

Some pictures, say a vase of flowers, do not have a background. In such cases your first cut will be around the outline of the whole image (the vase and flowers) and this layer will have to be mounted on a neutral base.

Always keep any spare bits of print until the end. You will be glad of them when, as frequently happens, you suddenly spot a further possibility for detailing that you had not noticed at the outset.

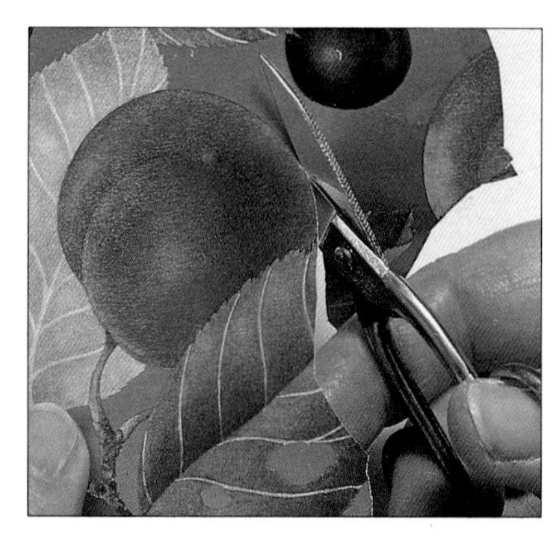

Cut around shapes with the middle of the scissors – turn the paper, not the scissors. Follow outlines closely. Avoid cutting curves as a series of straight lines. If you are right-handed, cut anti-clockwise so that you can always see the picture; if left-handed, cut clockwise.

Cutting with scissors

Small sharp nail scissors are best for cutting around the edges of each segment. You will use them a lot so they should fit your hand and feel comfortable. I prefer straight-bladed scissors as you cannot cut a straight line with the curved variety. On the other hand, curved blades can be easier on some shapes and angles.

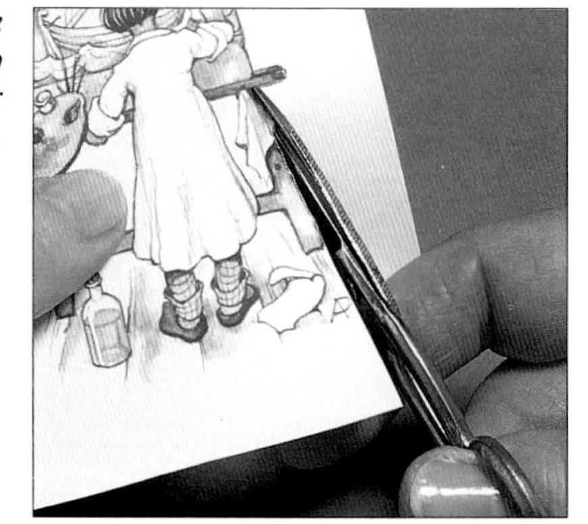

Use the points of the scissors to cut into tight corners and for very small pieces.

Over-cut into adjacent parts of the picture when, for example, the petals of a flower overlap.

Over-cutting

When cutting background pieces that will be partially hidden behind subsequent layers, for example, flower petals, do not cut along the line where the upper petal overlaps the lower one. Instead, include a small section of the adjacent area in the lower piece. That way, when the upper layer is positioned, there is no possibility of being able to see the edge of the lower piece.

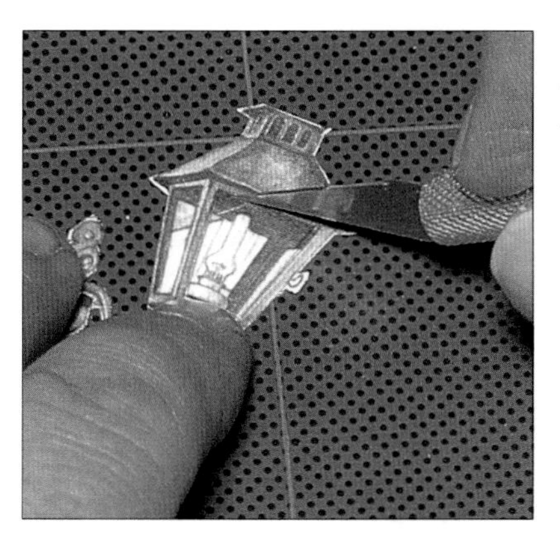

Use a craft knife and a cutting mat to cut intricate detail such as the pane of glass from this lamp.

Cutting with a craft knife

If you are cutting a piece from the centre of the print, use a craft knife. Do not cut from the edge of the print. This way you will not cut through something you may need later. A craft knife is also ideal for cutting intricate pieces such as panes of glass and spokes of wheels, and for the technique of 'feathering'.

Your blade should be straight and pointed (curved or hooked shapes are not suitable for this work). Again, it is essential that the cutting edge is sharp and you should change the blade as soon as it starts to drag.

You will want a ruler for measuring and for cutting straight lines. It can be dangerous to cut against a plastic ruler, so I recommend you use a steel-edged one.

You will also need a mat to cut on. Special self-healing mats for use with craft knives can be bought from most craft shops or suppliers. Some people use polystyrene or cork for their cutting surface but in my experience they are not so effective: polystyrene tends to break up and leave an uneven surface while cork grips the blade, making it difficult to cut.

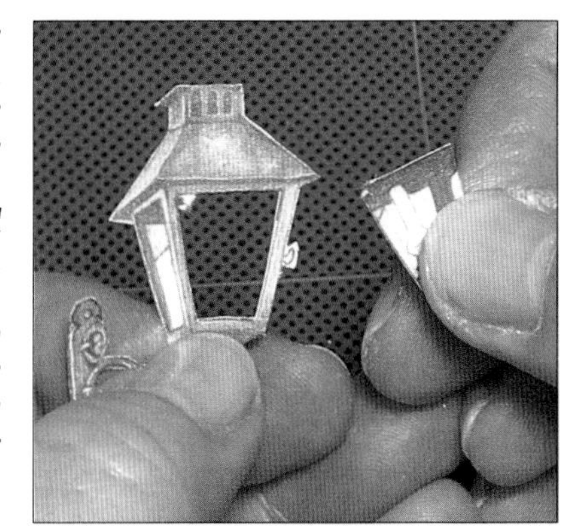

If your first cut does not go right through the paper, repeat the cut. Never pull the pieces apart: at best, you will leave a ragged edge; at worst, you will ruin the print. This applies both to using the craft knife and to using scissors to cut out a V-shape or right-angle.

Feathering

This cutting technique is used to accentuate feathers and hair: it can make birds and long-haired animals look very realistic but be sure to keep both the width and length of your cuts in proportion to the size of the subject. It is best done with a sharp craft knife on a cutting mat.

When feathering, first cut round the edge of the print piece and then make a series of small cuts of varying length into the picture at different angles.

Shading

No matter how careful you are, when you cut into a print or card you will always be left with a white edge which will detract from the finished result unless you do something about it. This can be disguised (shaded) simply by running a soft pencil (2B or 3B) around the edge. Felt-tip pens can be used but sometimes they bleed into the paper. Generally they will also give too dark an appearance, which can be just as distracting as the original problem.

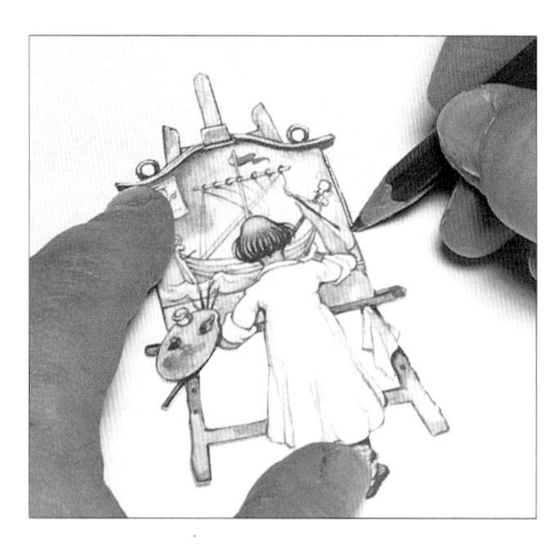

Use a soft pencil to shade the cut edges of each piece of the picture.

Shaping

Most pictures have an inbuilt perspective but you can give more life and realism to them by gently shaping some of the pieces. However, do remember that this will reduce the size of a piece relative to its flat image below, so do not distort a piece too much. If you have been over-enthusiastic, it is usually possible to reduce the curvature by applying gentle pressure to the centre of the piece. Always study flowers carefully and try to shape the petals in a natural manner.

Use this technique on the top layers of your picture. Of course, there is no point in shaping any piece which is actually a flat surface, nor any pieces which are covered by a subsequent layer: indeed, a flat surface gives a better base for the supporting blobs of adhesive.

I find the best 'tools' for shaping small pieces of paper are my fingers. However, for any larger pieces, a spoon with a rounded end on the handle will also come in useful. Place the piece face down on the cutting mat and work the end of the handle around the edges.

To emphasise creases in clothes or curtains, or to bring out the veins in a leaf, use the edge of the spoon handle. Mark the lines of the crease or vein on the back of the print with a pencil, place the piece face down on your cutting mat and gently run the edge of your spoon handle along the lines. When you turn the piece over, the crease or vein will stand out.

Alternatively, if you want the creases or veins to be concave, run the edge of the spoon down both sides of the pencil lines.

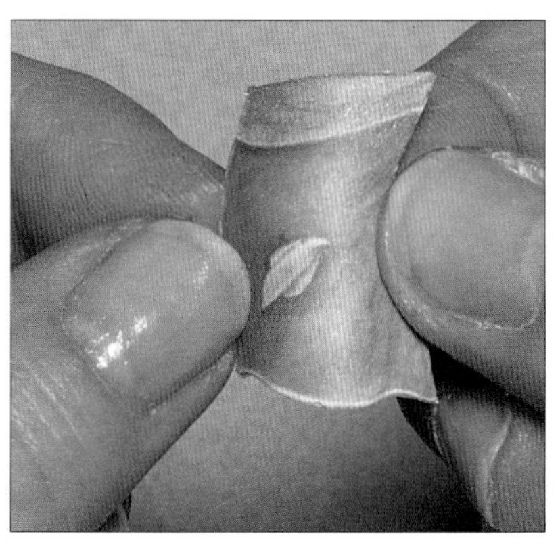

For rounded objects such as this coat, bend them over your finger until the amount of curve looks right.

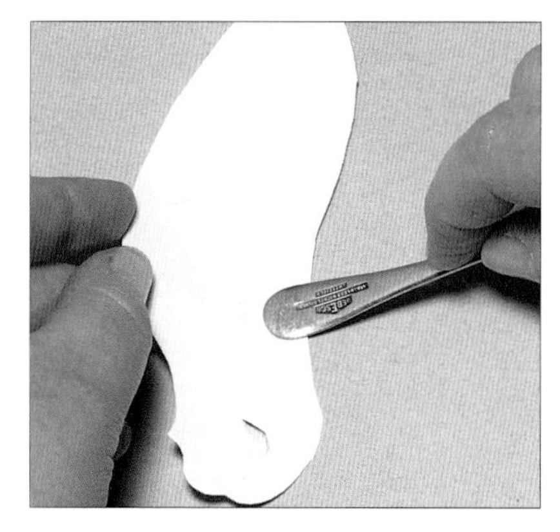

Use the rounded end of a spoon handle to shape large pieces.

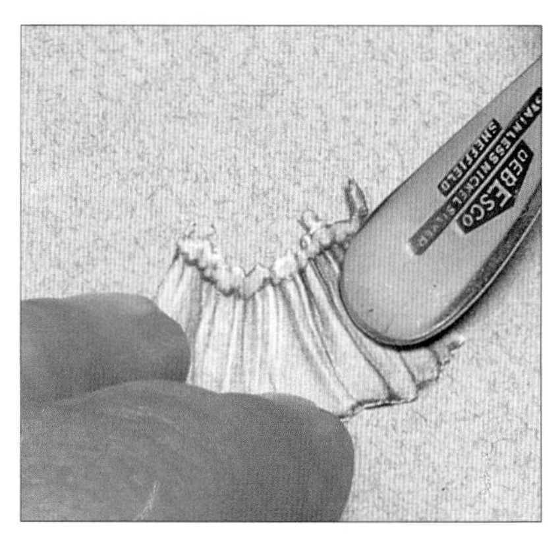

Use the edge of the spoon handle to emphasise creases.

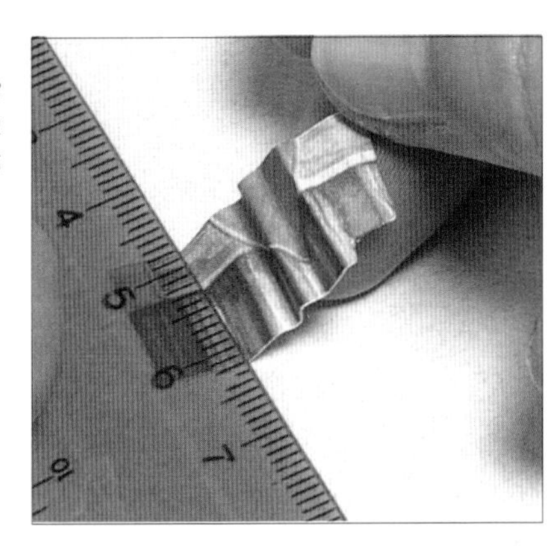

When shaping stairs, position a ruler on the bend line and then carefully lift the print against it.

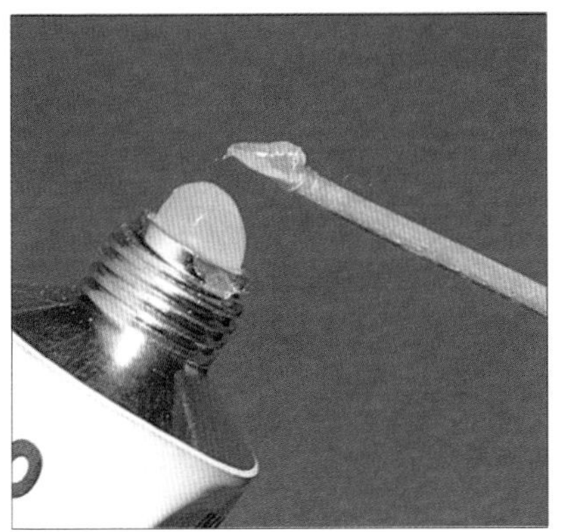

Use a cocktail stick to transfer small blobs of adhesive from the container to the picture.

Use a clean cocktail stick to nudge pieces into position.

As a general rule, keep the gap between each layer to about the thickness of a small coin.

To add realism to stairs, cut them out and then bend them against a straight edge, first one way, then the other (concertina-fashion), so that they mimic the shape of real stairs. Be careful not to mark the face of the print when doing this.

Gluing

I always use a silicone rubber adhesive to hold the different layers of the picture away from each other. This is very similar to the sealant used around baths and wash basins. It dries almost clear and has the advantage over other glues in that it does not run or shrink. It can therefore be used in blobs to keep the layers of your picture separate from yet attached to each other. It also takes about half an hour to dry, or cure, which gives you ample time to adjust the position of pieces as necessary. It can be obtained from most craft shops or découpage suppliers in different-sized tubes.

You can use self-adhesive pads to separate the layers of your picture (see page 42), but I find that adhesive is more versatile.

Always apply the adhesive to the base picture and not to the piece you are adding; that way there is less chance of getting the adhesive on your fingers. Follow the normal rules for handling adhesives: squeeze tubes from the bottom; always replace the lid between layers; and keep them out of reach of small children.

It is important to use just the right amount of adhesive – too little and you will not get the three-dimensional effect; but use too much and the foreground will look as though it is floating in mid-air.

For small areas, I find it best to use wooden cocktail sticks to transfer blobs of adhesive from the container on to the paper, especially when tiny amounts have to be positioned precisely.

Use another cocktail stick to nudge the pieces into place. Do not press too hard; you do not want to flatten the picture, nor do you want excess adhesive squeezed out. As a guide, a gap the thickness of a coin between layers is about right, but there is no need to be obsessive about this.

For larger areas, and for raising the front of floors or ceilings, the adhesive can be applied in larger blobs and squeezed directly from the tube. It may be necessary to use a double or even triple blob of adhesive. Just apply one blob on top of another, taking care not to press too hard.

Allow about half-hour intervals between layers, which gives you plenty of time to position the pieces and adjust them as necessary. Should some adhesive get in the wrong place, let it dry completely then gently rub it off. On many papers this will leave no trace of the error.

If you notice a badly placed piece after the silicone has cured, cut through the blobs with a craft knife. The remaining half blob of adhesive may peel off or a small fresh blob can be placed on top of the remains of the original fixing.

For large blobs, dispense the adhesive straight from the tube. Build up blobs to get the correct height.

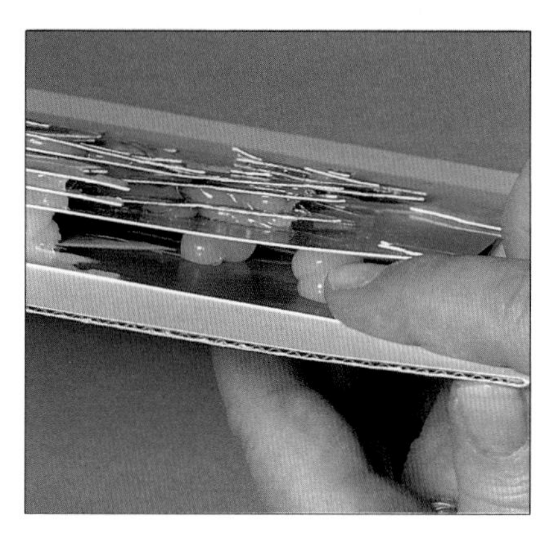

Use large or multiple blobs of adhesive to lift the foreground of a picture and accentuate the perspective.

Building the picture

The backing board on which you mount your picture should be the same size as the frame you are going to use. If the picture has a surround or border, your first decision has to be whether or not to keep it. I usually remove it and cover the backing board with neutral-coloured card.

Position your base picture in the middle of the board and secure it with a double-sided adhesive sheet or with glue (I find latex glue suitable).

If the picture is complicated or if you have a limited number of prints, cut out all the pieces before you start to assemble it. Ensure that you can detail all the main areas to a reasonable level.

Use a small pair of tweezers for picking up and positioning the pieces of your picture.

When building up the layers of the picture, do not make them too deep. Too much depth on small pictures starts to look less realistic.

The wall, ceiling and floor pieces of a room should be mounted so that they touch the base print at the furthest point. Build them up using increasingly larger blobs of adhesive towards the outer edges. Similarly, in a street scene the road and the buildings should be built up from the centre towards the outer edges of the picture.

Cover the backing board with coloured card and then position the first layer of the picture in the middle.

Use a pair of tweezers for picking up small pieces of a picture.

Angle people out at the top so that their feet appear to touch the ground.

Open doors should give the appearance of being attached at their hinged edge but the open edge should stand proud.

People and animals must be angled outwards at the top so that their feet appear to touch the ground and their heads and bodies stand proud.

Varnishing

Let the varnish flow from the brush.

Painting on several coats of varnish will harden your picture and help to protect it from light. However, never hang pictures in direct sunlight as in time they may fade. Bottles of suitable varnish can be bought from any découpage print supplier. Varnish is best applied with a soft brush which will minimise the formation of bubbles. Keep a separate brush for dusting your picture before you start varnishing and between coats.

Apply the varnish to a small area at a time. I find that several thin coats are better than one or two thick ones and I usually use six to eight. However, do not try to brush out the varnish as you would with household paint. Instead, use the brush to encourage the varnish to flow evenly over the area to be covered.

Place the varnished picture in an old cardboard box to keep it free of dust while it dries.

Allow the varnish to dry completely between coats and keep it clear of dust and dirt (I use nothing fancier than a old cardboard box covered with a newspaper). Always keep your picture flat while drying to avoid runs.

You do not have to varnish the whole picture – sometimes you can leave the background matt to emphasise the impression of depth further.

Do take your time when applying the varnish – by this stage you will have put in too much effort to risk spoiling it by hurrying. Finally, make sure that you clean your brush thoroughly after use; if you do not, your next effort may well be spoilt by dust-like deposits.

Mounting and framing

Having taken the time and effort to create your three-dimensional picture, you really ought to frame it or have it framed for you. I like to use ready-made frames and I show you how I use them on page 46.

Using prints

Making flower pictures

Flowers are perhaps the most popular subject for three-dimensional découpage. If you start with a simple subject such as a pansy, a poppy or the anemones shown below, you can then progress to larger and more complicated arrangements.

1

a. Cut round the complete outline of the flowers and leaves on the first print.

b. From the second print, cut round the outline of the mauve flower (over-cutting at the left to include part of the large red flower), the complete small red flower, and the centre part of the large red one.

c. Now use the third, fourth and fifth prints to cut out the pieces as shown.

Anemones

Print size: 76 x 76mm (3 x 3in)

This small print is typical of the many pictures of flower arrangements that are ideal subjects for the beginner. Having studied this picture, I decided to have two layers of the leaves behind the bottom red flower, four layers of petals on each flower and a separate layer of their centre parts. By careful cutting I managed to get all the shapes from just five copies of the picture. The small red flower overlaps the leaves, and the large red flower overlaps the mauve one, so I over-cut some of the pieces to allow for this. Note that the shapes are not cut out in the same order as they are assembled.

2

Using a soft pencil and a piece of scrap paper, shade all the cut edges.

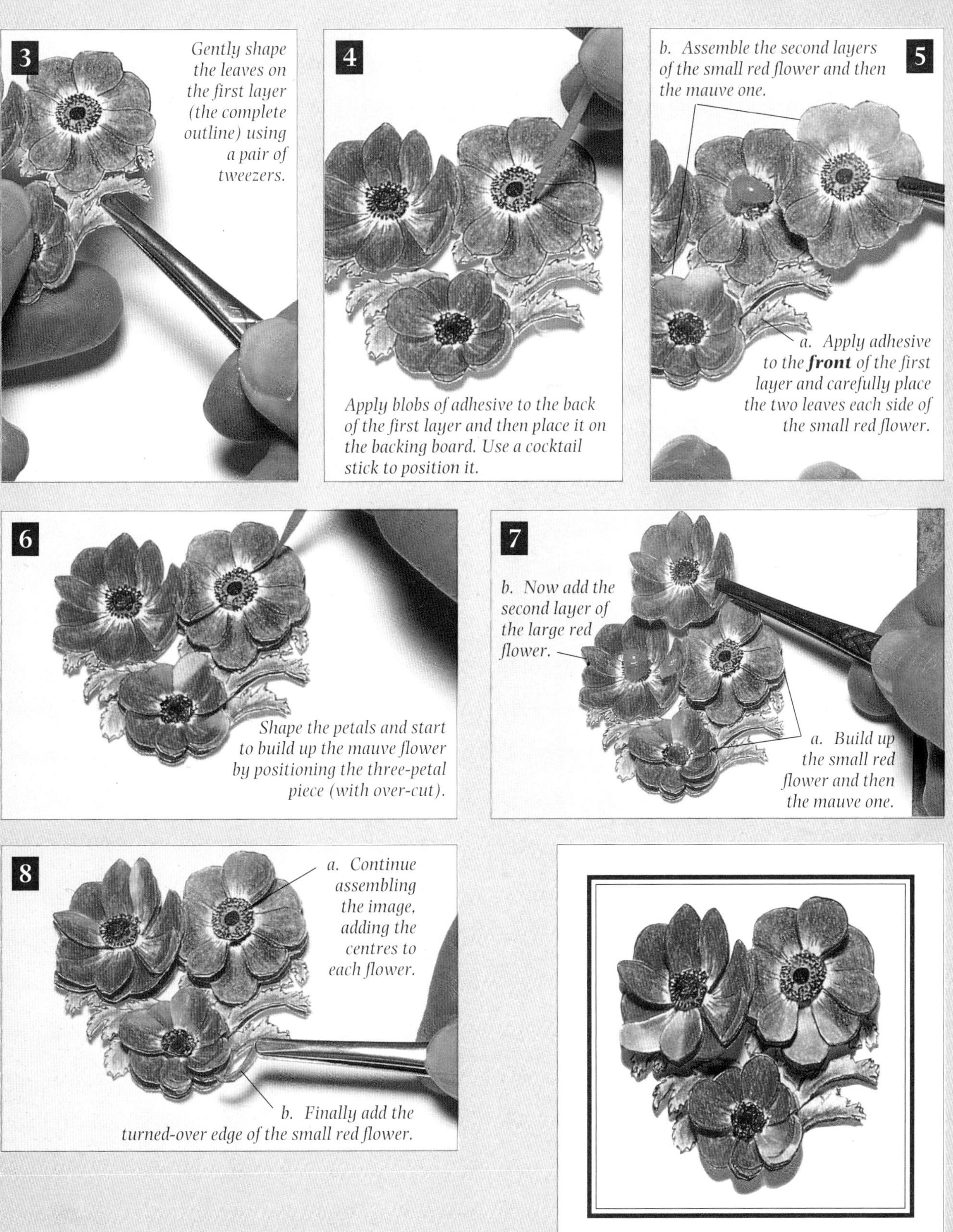

The finished three-dimensional picture.

Fuchsia

Print size 125 x 148mm (5 x 5¾in)

Fuchsias are lovely flowers and care should be taken to shape the petals correctly. The stamens, cut as a group from the second print, are shaped to hang at different levels. The pale pink outer petals (sepals) of the main flower have to be shaped so that they curve outwards and upwards; their bottom edges must touch the lower layer while the top of each petal stands proud. The inner petals (corollas) curve outwards and downwards; they must touch at the top and stand proud at the bottom.

Do not forget the small details on the picture, such as the dew-drops on the petals – they may be fiddly to cut out, but they do make all the difference to the finished picture.

Pansies

Print size 200 x 150mm (8 x 6in)

Six prints were used to create this arrangement. Some of the leaves have only two layers but the leaf in the centre foreground has six. Varying the number of layers gives more depth and realism to the picture. The original ground was similar to that of the cyclamen on the front cover, but I decided to eliminate this and to mount just the arrangement on a black background to accentuate the delicate colours.

Making pictures with character studies

There are a lot of wonderful character studies that lend themselves to three-dimensional découpage. Use the shaping techniques to emphasise the shape of clothing and any rounded objects in the picture. Really study the image and use different layers to highlight details such as handkerchiefs, frills, shoes and shoe laces, shirt collars and cuffs, etc. Lay down parts of limbs at an angle, rather than flat, to accentuate the perspective.

The painter

Print size 76 x 133mm (3 x 5¼in)

This picture, by the Dutch artist Anton Pieck, is one of a number of his works that are favourites with three-dimensional découpage artists. All of his paintings include a great amount of detail and they allow you to achieve good results from a minimum number of prints.

Before starting to cut, study the picture closely and consider which parts are nearest the back and which are closest to you.

In this picture there are three basic features: the easel, the canvas mounted on the easel and the painter himself. There are also a number of details that can be accentuated: the sketch pinned to the top of the canvas; the palette; the cloth hanging from the easel; the bottle and the piece of paper on the floor.

Having planned the basic structure, I found that I only needed six prints: one to use as the base picture (the complete image) and five from which to cut the detail (see right). Note the details of the turn-ups on the painter's trousers and the turned-over edge of the piece of paper on the floor, cut from the sixth print.

Print 1

Print 2

Print 3

Print 4

Print 5

Print 6

The parts of the picture you will need to cut from the six prints.

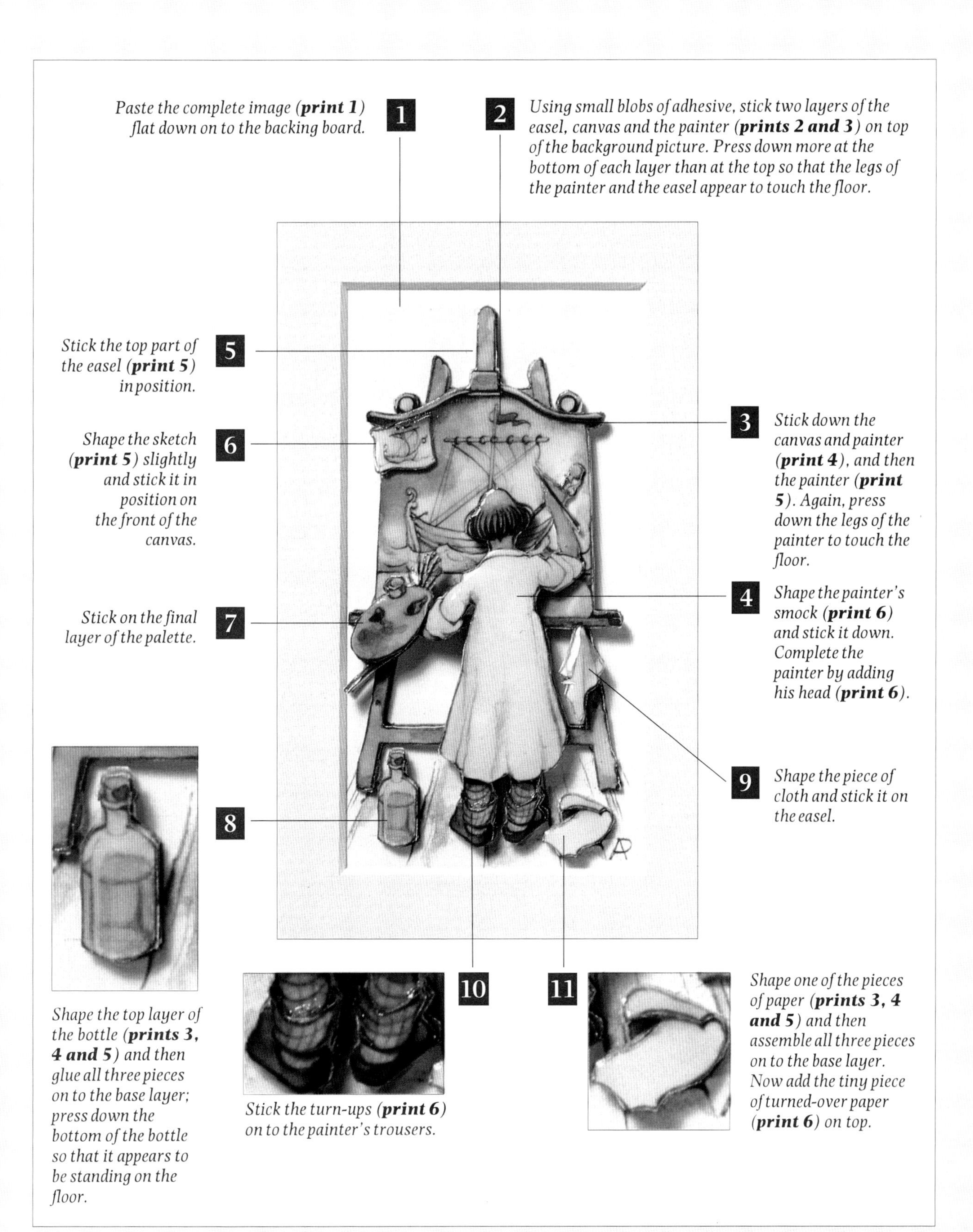
1
Paste the complete image (**print 1**) flat down on to the backing board.
2
Using small blobs of adhesive, stick two layers of the easel, canvas and the painter (**prints 2 and 3**) on top of the background picture. Press down more at the bottom of each layer than at the top so that the legs of the painter and the easel appear to touch the floor.
3
Stick down the canvas and painter (**print 4**), and then the painter (**print 5**). Again, press down the legs of the painter to touch the floor.
4
Shape the painter's smock (**print 6**) and stick it down. Complete the painter by adding his head (**print 6**).
5
Stick the top part of the easel (**print 5**) in position.
6
Shape the sketch (**print 5**) slightly and stick it in position on the front of the canvas.
7
Stick on the final layer of the palette.
8
Shape the top layer of the bottle (**prints 3, 4 and 5**) and then glue all three pieces on to the base layer; press down the bottom of the bottle so that it appears to be standing on the floor.
9
Shape the piece of cloth and stick it on the easel.
10
Stick the turn-ups (**print 6**) on to the painter's trousers.
11
Shape one of the pieces of paper (**prints 3, 4 and 5**) and then assemble all three pieces on to the base layer. Now add the tiny piece of turned-over paper (**print 6**) on top.

The blacksmith

Print size 76 x 133mm (3 x 5¼in)
This picture is in the same series as Anton Pieck's *The Painter* and it is made up in much the same way from six prints. However, in this case, I included part of the floor in the second layer, and I used large blobs of adhesive to angle the floor downwards from the front to the back. This emphasises the depth of the scene and allows the blacksmith's clogs to stand firmly on the ground.

Shape the head of the hammer to make it look solid.

Shape two layers of the leather apron and press the outer points of it together to accentuate its fullness.

Include part of the floor in the second layer and use larger blobs of adhesive to angle it up at the front.

The blacksmith's neck only appears on the second and third layers.

Shape the anvil to accentuate the horizontal surface.

Cut out the tiny details (the clogs, the hammer head, the horse-shoes, the pocket, and the blacksmith's right hand from the final print.

The piano girl

Print size 76 x 133mm (3 x 5¼in)
Yet another one of Anton Pieck's pictures – again, a simple scene that can be cut out and assembled in distinct layers.

The cellist *(opposite)*

Print size 152 x 198mm (6 x 7¾in)
This is a very good picture from which to work up a three-dimensional image. It has very definite lines around which you can cut and, when you study it, you will see lots of layers that you can add. Take the man's clothes, for example: the lapel of his coat, the body of the coat, the forearms, the cuffs of his shirt, the handkerchief, the bow tie, the shirt collar and the row of buttons can all be accentuated.

Again, because of the sharp definitions you can give some treatment to the man's face. I used four layers: one of the complete head; one without the mouth and chin; one without his moustache and the hair at the right-hand side; and, finally, one of the strands of hair and his eyebrows and nose.

Seven copies of the print were used to make this three-dimensional picture.

The facial details were worked from four prints of the picture. Slits were cut under the eyelids, which were then shaped with a pair of tweezers.

The forearm of the coat, the cuff of the shirt and the musician's hand were cut from different prints. A craft knife was used to separate the fingers, which were then shaped around the bow.

The rest was cut as a single layer and angled down slightly so that it appears to touch the floor.

The socks, trousers, shoes, laces and the toecaps of the shoes are all different layers.

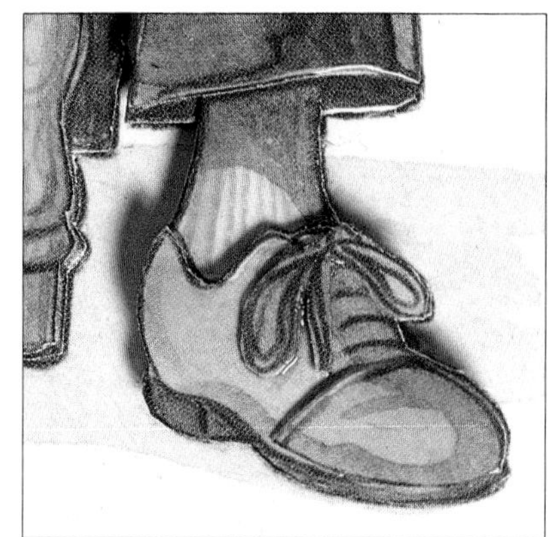

Cutting intricate detail

When you have got used to the basic techniques of cutting and building up simple pictures you can start to work on more intricate ones. Street scenes, such as the example on this page, give you the opportunity to expand your new-found skills of developing a flat image into a three-dimensional picture. Again, study the picture carefully and make notes about the different levels that you can see in the picture.

The toy shop

Print size 222 x 152mm (8¾ x 6in)

This is a very good picture to work on: it has a lot of intricate detail, which needs very careful cutting, and it has a number of different levels.

The interior of the shop is the lowest level – you can include sub-levels for the beam, the toys on the shelves, the old gentleman, the toy yacht and the open door.

The next level is the ground-floor front wall of the building, with sub-levels for the small window at the right and the many toys fixed to the wall.

Coming forward, the bow window offers the opportunity of using a number of sub-levels for all the toys.

The huge wooden beams that support the upper floor of the building can be shaped to accentuate their solidity. Use more layers for the shop sign and the lamp.

The cobbled street and pavement can be angled upwards and outwards to enhance the perspective in the picture (see also page 26).

Finally, the lady, the perambulator, the dog, the small girl and the rocking horse can all be built up in layers to complete the picture.

Of course, you can work as much detail and as many layers as you want, but remember that your decision will affect the number of prints that you will need.

This example was made with eight prints.

Take great care when cutting out window panes like these. The thin lines of the wooden frame need delicate handling if they are to remain intact.

The undersides of the large beams are angled outward with large blobs of adhesive. The beam itself is cut from another print and layered on top. The shop sign is made from three separate layers of paper.

This lamp is made up from two levels of paper. The lower one, which shows the interior of the lamp, is creased along the line that separates the front and left-hand side. The upper layer is cut to leave just the front and top of the lamp.

This doorway may seem an insignificant part of the picture, but if you give it the right treatment, it comes to life and adds more interest to the finished work. Apart from the base picture there are ten separate pieces of paper in this part of the picture.

These wheels also need very careful cutting. The far-side pair of wheels are cut as one piece, together with the handle and body of the perambulator. This piece is glued down so that the wheels touch the angled street level. The near-side pair of wheels are cut as individual circles and glued so that they are just proud of the street and slightly higher at the top.

Creating depth

Every picture has an inbuilt perspective, with the objects that are furthest away from the eye being smaller than those in the foreground. Cutting out and then layering different levels will enhance the depth of the picture by a certain amount, but you can accentuate it even more by angling parts of the picture downwards and inwards from the outer edges, by using different-sized blobs of adhesive.

The photographer

Print size 222 x 152mm ($8\frac{3}{4}$ x 6in)

This picture, in keeping with most of the artist's work, has a considerable amount of detail that you can use to good effect. In addition, the room setting has a floor, ceiling and walls that can be angled in towards the centre to increase the depth.

There are a number of distinct levels in the painting, each of which can be accentuated with sub-levels of detail. At the back, behind the arch, is the entrance to the studio. On the right-hand side, the stairwell can be set back behind the newel post. The portraits on the back wall can be layered. The beams on the ceiling and the old gas lamp can be shaped and layered as a sub-level. The individual characters in the painting can all be treated as sub-levels. Finally, the items in the foreground, the kettle on the stove and the photographs on the table can be lifted clear of the floor.

I used eight prints to complete this picture.

Add detail to the foreground objects. This old kettle is made from three separate pieces, each of which is shaped to show the roundness of the kettle.

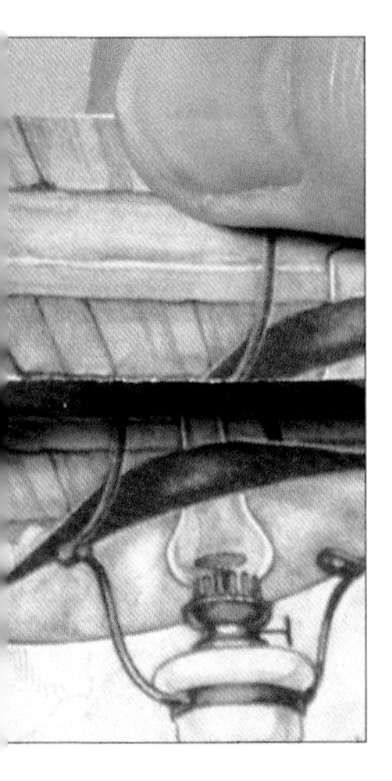

This piece of the ceiling is angled upwards, from back to front, using different-sized blobs of adhesive. The same technique is used for the backdrop behind the sitter and for the floor. The beams are cut out as individual pieces, shaped and then added to this layer.

The statue and newel post are raised well away from the staircase wall to make the wall recede into the background. The stairs are made by shaping the paper like a concertina as shown on page 13.

Monaco Grand Prix

Print size: 180 x 130mm (7 x 5in)

Landscape pictures must be selected with care but you can get some stunning results.

In this picture there are three distinct background levels: the buildings; the boats, spectators and the safety fence; and the surface of the track. In the foreground there are also separate levels; Nigel Mansell in his racing car and Ayrton Senna in his. Each of these five levels can be built up with a number of sub-levels to create a really good three-dimensional image. I used eight prints to make the example shown here, but by careful cutting I have in fact been able to make many more layers.

Work from the back and gradually build up the layers, slightly increasing the angle of each sub-layer to enhance the perspective.

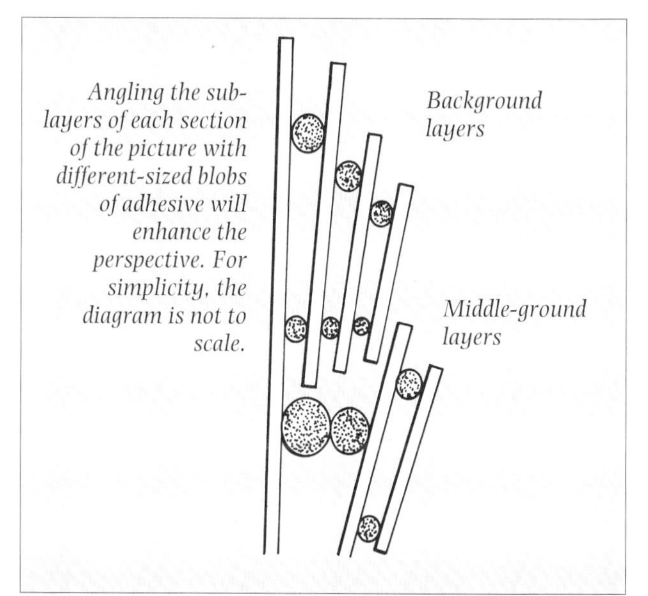

Angling the sub-layers of each section of the picture with different-sized blobs of adhesive will enhance the perspective. For simplicity, the diagram is not to scale.

Tangmere trio

Print size: 180 x 130mm (7 x 5in)

Again I used eight prints for this picture. The cliffs are cut into three layers and are angled upwards at the top to lift them clear of the distant sea. Large blobs of adhesive are used to bring the bottom edge right away from the base print (see page 14).

The clouds, apart from the one in the centre foreground (which is made from two layers), are cut as single layers of card. The large ones to the left are angled upwards at the top to lift them away from the cliffs.

The three aeroplanes are made from different numbers of layers of paper to complement their relative size and detail. The nearest one has five layers, the middle one has four and the small one only three.

Use even-sized blobs of adhesive to angle the first layer of the cliffs upwards at the top to lift them clear of the distant sea.

Feathering

Pictures of birds and animals can look rather plain if you simply cut round their outlines and layer the various levels. Use the feathering technique (see page 11) to improve their visual appearance. You can also enhance the shapes of some of the larger feathers by slicing between pairs of them and then, using a pair of tweezers, carefully angling the feathers away from each other.

Owl in winter

Print size 125 x 175mm (5 x 7in)

The feathering technique is used extensively on the head and legs of this owl. The picture also has lots of other intricate detail, in the form of leaves, twigs and icicles, on which to practise your skills.

Shape the ivy leaves and build up layers to increase depth. Cut and glue the bricks as single layers just proud of the mortar.

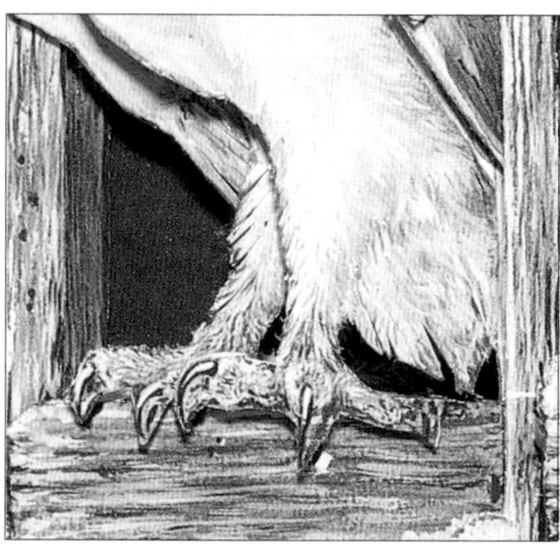

The feathering technique adds shape and texture to the picture.

Build up the snow- covered logs and the trailing ivy. Angle the dead twigs downwards at the top so they contact the wall.

Shape the windowsill and then glue down the snow as two layers, with the icicles on the front layer standing above the level of the sill.

Kingfishers

Print size 125 x 175mm (5 x 7in)

I cut the second print of this picture along the horizon line and then used large blobs of adhesive to angle the area of water outwards at the bottom.

I used the slicing and shaping technique on the outer wing feathers of the bird in flight and the feathering technique on all the other pieces. I feathered various layers of the bird perched on the log and used the slicing technique on the tips of its wings. I also cut small V-shapes round some of the tips of the feathers on the inner part of the wing and then lifted the points slightly to give some depth to the bird.

Again, small details, such as the fisherman's float, help to give depth all over the image. Use just one layer of the print, shape it to enhance its roundness and angle it out at the top.

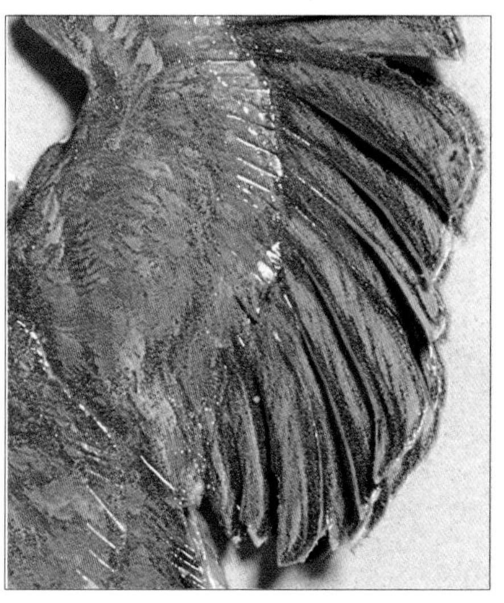

Slice between pairs of flight feathers and use a pair of tweezers to angle each feather away from its neighbour.

Cut small V-shapes around individual wing feathers and use the tip of a craft knife to lift them clear of the wing.

Using colour photocopies

You do not have to limit your skills to working with commercial sets of prints – you can produce some very satisfactory results from other types of printed image. Nowadays, there are lots of high-street print shops where you can get colour photocopies of your favourite pictures.

Now, normal photocopying paper is rather thin and flimsy, and some will become translucent when the adhesive is applied. However, if you ask for your prints to be made on a heavy, good-quality paper you should find that it will be all right. Try and get a sample of the paper and experiment with the adhesive.

Colour photocopies are slightly more expensive than the normal prints but you will have a picture that is not readily available to others.

On these and the following two pages I have included some examples of pictures copied in this way. The colours are very good and quite true to the original prints.

There is lots of detail in the top right-hand corner, which will allow you to create real depth in the picture.

Wild cats

Print size: 165 x 155mm (6½ x 6in)

This picture shows a leopard swimming in a pool of water. Water is a subject which usually creates problems because of undefined edges, but in this case there is a distinct line between the body of the leopard and its reflection in the water.

I used two complete prints for the background: one I glued down flat as a base picture; the other one, with a slot cut along the reflection line, I angled in an increasing curve from the top to the bottom with varying sizes of adhesive blobs.

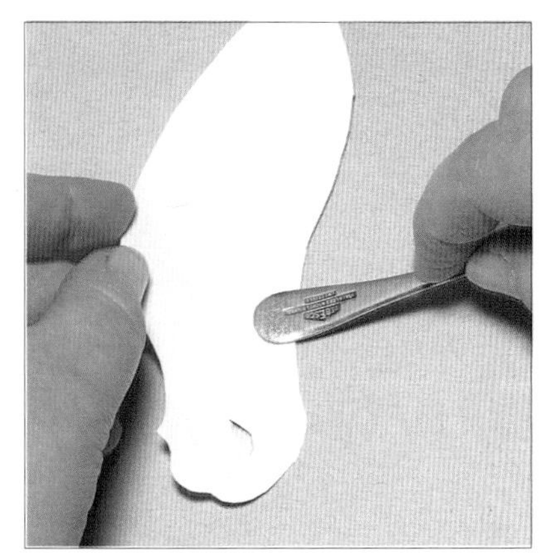

Use the rounded end of a spoon handle to shape the top layer of the swimming leopard.

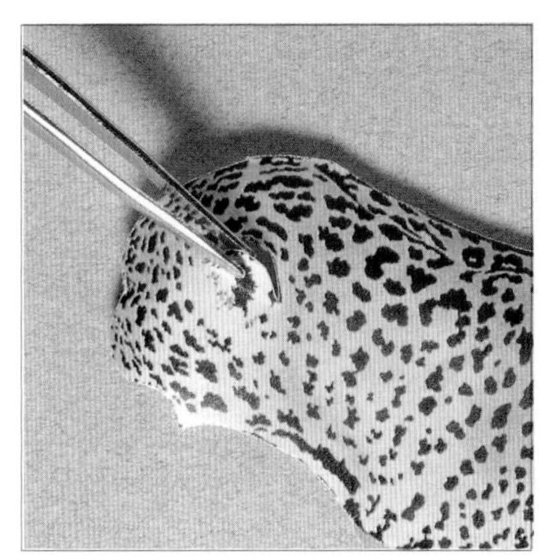

Cut round the ear and then carefully bend the ear forward so that it is slightly proud of the body. Note that I have omitted the nose from this top layer to accentuate the shape of the head.

Over-cut each of the three layers of the body to include part of the reflection, and slide them into a slot in the second (final) layer of the water.

The finished picture.

Exotic birds

Print size: 180 x 130mm (7 x 5in)

The very vivid colours attracted me to this picture of parrots and hornbills that I found in a book on silk painting. I thought it had potential for three-dimensional treatment, and I got my local printer to make me six colour photocopies.

I used a small amount of feathering technique on the red tail feathers of the blue parrot, and I also sliced and shaped most of the wing feathers of all the birds. There is quite a lot of shaping in the leaves to emphasise their curves and the way they overlap each other.

Fantasy horses

Print size: 185 x 192mm (7¼ x 7½in)

This is quite a simple picture, but one that comes to life with the three-dimensional treatment. Again it is made from six colour photocopies printed on good-quality paper. I shaped the bodies of all the horses to give them some bulk and I then went to town shaping and layering their manes and tails.

Using photographs

Photographs are another source material that you can try, but you will have to choose the subject with care.

Landscapes which have clearly defined edges are best, but, although some portraits work quite well, you will have problems with the soft edges of facial detail. However, if you do have a favourite photograph that brings back happy memories, it is well worth experimenting with it.

Normal photographic paper is rather thick, so you will have to make a point of shading the cut edges. You must also take care when shaping – the glossy surface of normal prints can resist bending, but you can use different-sized blobs of adhesive to hold the shape. Some photographic dealers can supply matt prints on a thinner paper, which will help with both of these problems.

Devil's Peak, Cape Town

Print size: 180 x 130mm (7 x 5in)

This photograph of Cape Town, with the large building in the foreground, the suburbs in the middle ground and the mountains at the back, is an ideal subject for three-dimensional découpage.

I used six prints to make this example. One complete print forms the base layer and the other five prints were cut through the middle ground. This enabled me to have five layers for the mountain and five basic layers for the middle and foreground. I also cut out some of the small foreground pieces from the lower layers of the bottom half of the picture to allow me to include a lot of detail on the nearest buildings. The sections were layered much like the Grand Prix cars on page 28.

Ancient temple, Delphi, Greece

Print size: 180 x 130mm (7 x 5in)

The subject of this photograph is ideal for three-dimensional treatment. It has a soft background but very sharp edges to the columns and the rocks in the foreground.

The happy couple

Print size: 130 x 180mm (5 x 7in)

This was a rather difficult subject to work with but I have included it to show that you can use some of your favourite snaps to good effect. Faces, with their soft edges, have to be treated as a single layer but you can cut, shape and layer the clothing and limbs.

Using rubber stamps

Three-dimensional cards or pictures can be made using several rubber-stamp images and some colouring pens. The paper needs to be of good quality and pure white. Felt-tipped pens are good for colouring and you can decorate your picture with gold and silver pens, and with glitter.

Snow scene

This winter scene was made using four rubber-stamped images which were coloured identically, and then cut into layers.

I cut out the first image in full and used this as the base print. Note that I left some of the branches white to indicate the snow on them.

I omitted the trees and the chimneys on the second layer. I shaped the main part of the house by bending back the left-hand side and by creasing the centre of the roof slightly concave.

The third layer comprises the front part of the house. I cut a slit where the porch roof joins the wall at the right to allow me to bend the roof backwards at the top to emphasise its slope.

The fourth layer only includes the fence, the lamp and the foreground snow; I used a craft knife to cut out the spaces in the fence.

Finally, before I built up the picture I put a little glue on the snow-covered areas and sprinkled fine glitter over it to make it sparkle.

You can use rubber stamps to create any number of identical images which you can then use to create three-dimensional pictures. This type of work is ideal for all sorts of greetings cards.

Using gift wrap and tags

Gift wrap can also be used to make three-dimensional pictures provided that it is of good quality and weight, and has a repeat image. If the paper is too thin it may not hold any shaping and it may crack if you try to shape it too much. In addition, silicone adhesive may be visible through the paper. Metallic papers are not really suitable for similar reasons. Gift tags can also be built up if they are not too thick. If they have a hole in them with a cord, they can be used as unusual Christmas decorations. It is well worth the effort to try this source of material, and I have included a few examples to give you an idea of what you can achieve.

Robin *(opposite)*

The leaves in this picture were shaped by marking a line down the centre and then bending them along this line. I tried to feather the robin but this proved difficult because the paper was quite thin. I have to admit that it took two attempts for me to get a reasonable result.

Teddies in the snow *(opposite)*

These teddies were cut out and then built up individually. The snowballs were difficult to shape – I overcame this problem by putting a large blob of glue under the centre of each and tiny spots of glue round the edges. I then carefully shaped the pieces with my tweezers when the balls were placed in position.

Geese *(below left)*

Here is a typical example of one of the problems associated with the use of thin paper – the adhesive blobs have marked the white (unprinted) parts of the image. They were not evident when I assembled the picture, but gradually became more visible with time.

For interest's sake, the picture has five main parts: the first is the complete picture; the second is just the two geese; the third omits the back feet of the geese; the fourth layer comprises the wings and the necks of the geese, omitting their bills; and the final layer builds up the holly and the bows.

The single goose (below right) was made from a set of six gift tags that came with the wrapping paper. The thicker paper does not allow the adhesive to penetrate.

Using coloured paper

Three-dimensional découpage does not have to be restricted to pre-printed images. You can convert a simple drawing into a three-dimensional image using sheets of different-coloured paper. It is a good way to introduce children to this craft, and on these pages I show you, step by step, how to make such a picture. Instead of silicone rubber adhesive, I have used double-sided sticky pads to separate the layers of paper.

The drawing should be quite simple and include enclosed outlines which can be cut into different layers of colour. Small detail can be added with coloured pencils or marker pens.

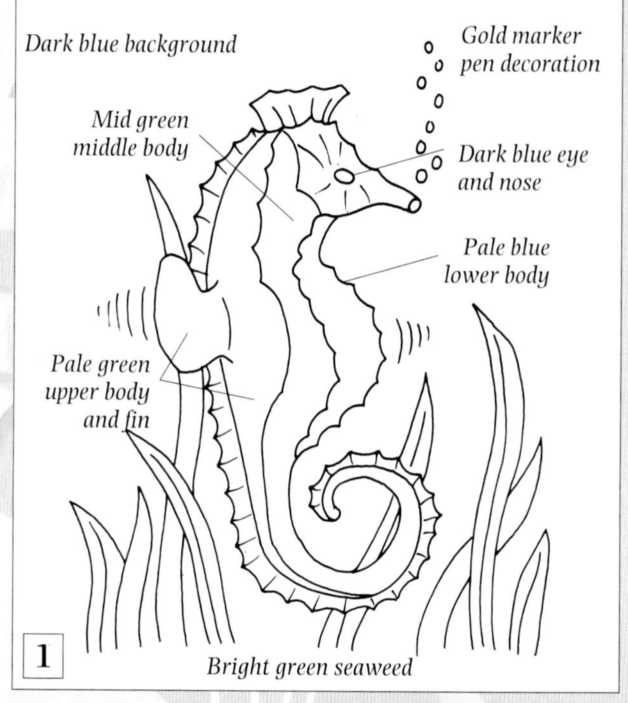

Draw a simple design (you could use one of the children's own pictures as an original) and decide on a suitable colour plan.

Copy the outline of each layer on to tracing paper and then trace them on to the appropriate sheet of coloured paper.

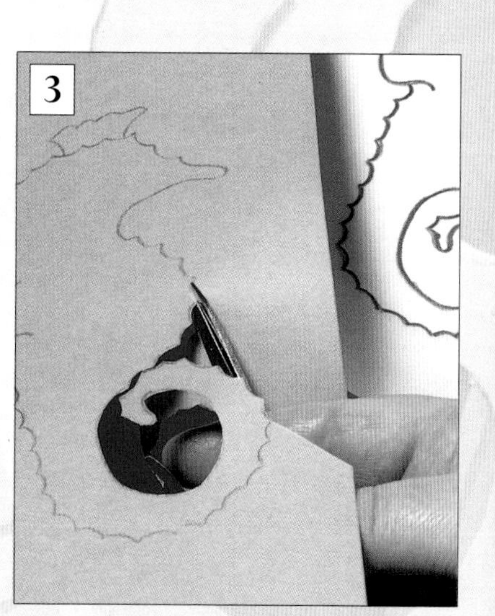

Use the middle of the scissors to cut round the pencil lines.

Use a marker pen to add the decoration.

Continue to trace and cut out all the segments of the picture.

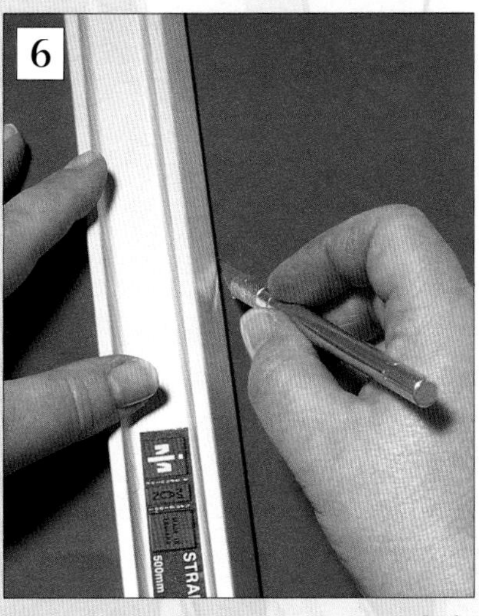

Use a craft knife to cut out a rectangle for the background.

Cut thin strips from the sheet of double-sided sticky pad.

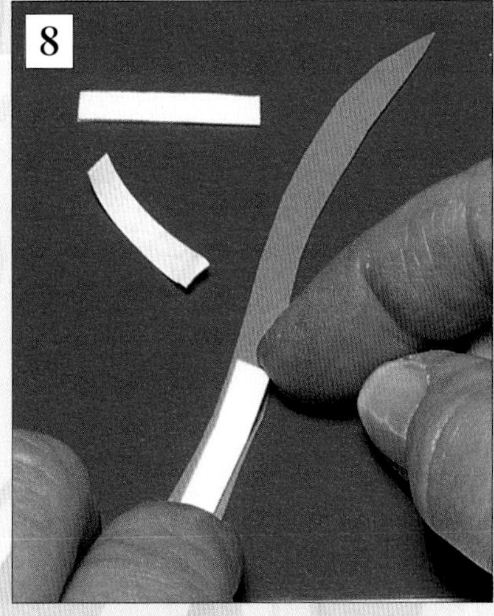

Stick a strip of sticky pad on to the back of the first leaf section.

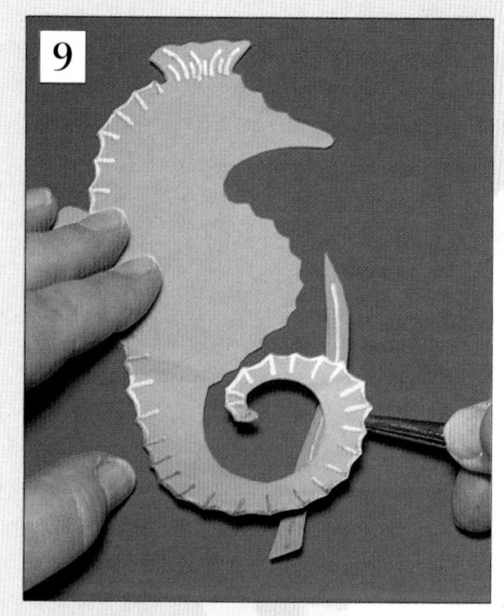

Hold the pale-blue body of the sea-horse over the background and place the first piece of seaweed in position behind it.

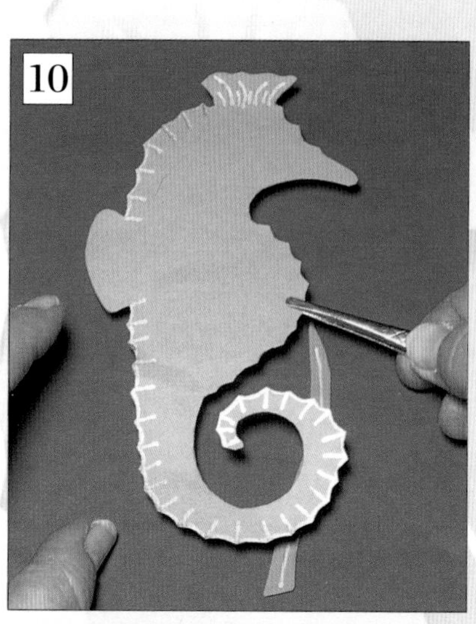

Add sticky pads to the back of the lower body and position it on the background, overlapping the first piece of seaweed.

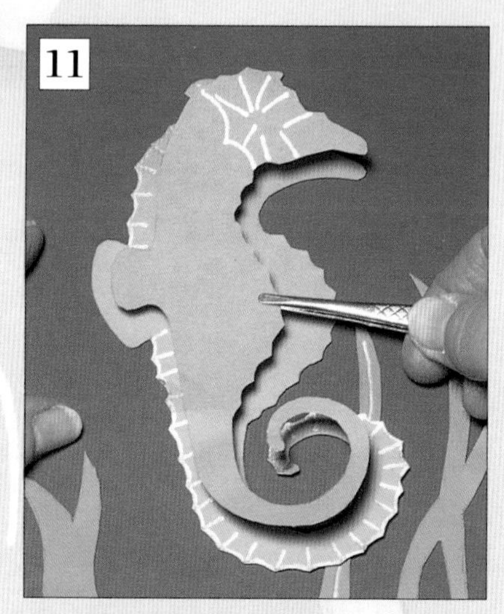

Complete the first layer of seaweed and then stick down the middle body of the sea-horse.

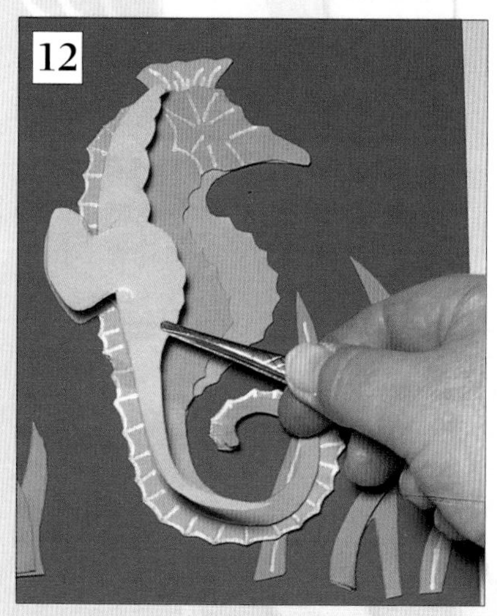

Now stick down the upper body piece in position.

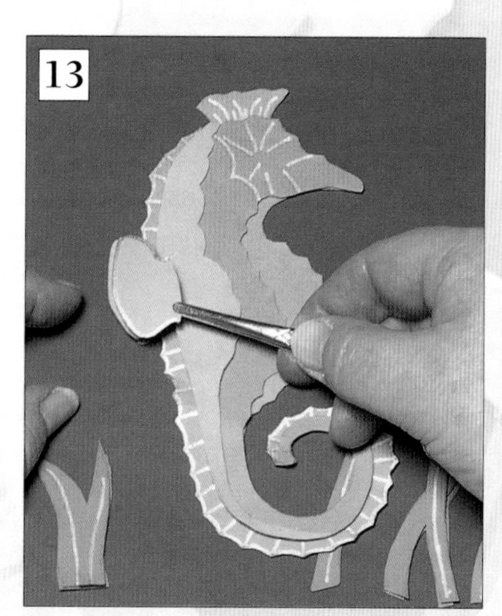

Add the fin.

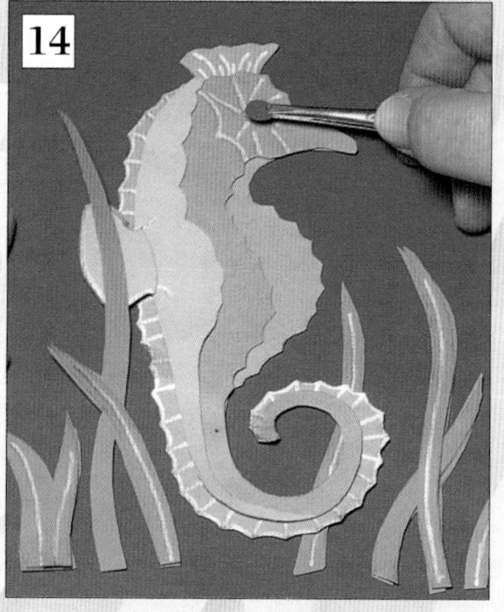

Complete the layering by sticking down the other pieces of seaweed followed by the nose and the eye of the sea-horse.

Finally, add the bubbles and the other decoration on the background with the gold marker.

Mounting and framing your work

Having spent the time and effort to create a three-dimensional picture it is worth completing the job properly by mounting and framing it.

Mounts

Unless you invest in special cutting equipment, mounts are best obtained from your local picture framer. They are not that expensive, and a proper mount with a bevelled edge will look far better than one cut with a scalpel. There are many colours to choose from and you can add a touch of individuality by drawing in one or more lines around the aperture – gold lines look great against a dark colour, for example. Try using double or triple mounts in contrasting or complementary colours; they can look superb with a large picture.

Frames

Découpage print suppliers often sell ready-made, deep-rebate frames for three-dimensional pictures. The deep rebate allows the use of fillets to keep the front of the picture away from the glass. Using one of these is the easiest way to frame your picture, but you are limited in the choice of frame material and they are not cheap.

I tend to use ordinary frames into which I build my own rebate from sheets of foam-core board, which is stiff but light in weight. The rebate does stick out at the back but it is not visible when the picture is hung. If you keep your eyes open, you can buy frames quite cheaply. For instance, my local newspaper has regular advertisements for picture frame sales.

Cut four strips of foam-core board, making their width slightly more than the depth of your picture. Their lengths should be such that they fit (box-like) inside the frame; cut the longest sides first, then cut the other two sides to fit the gap between.

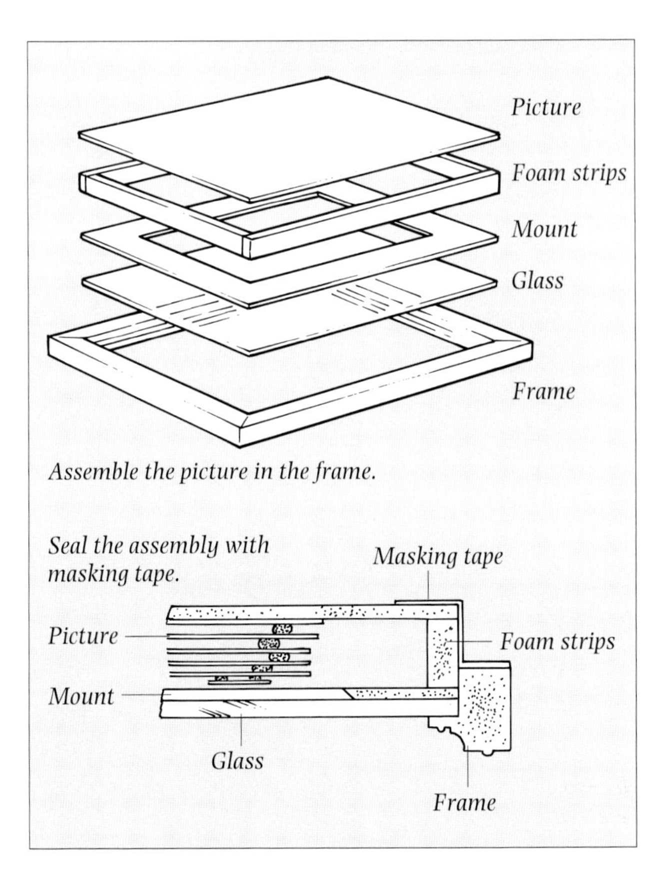

Assemble the picture in the frame.

Seal the assembly with masking tape.

Attach the strips to the inside of the frame with general-purpose adhesive and put aside to dry .

Place your finished picture on the edges of the foam board and secure it to the board with masking tape. An overlapping layer of tape will cover the foam board and help secure it to the frame.

Attach eyelet screws to the back of the sides of the frame about one-third down from the top and tie picture-framing wire straight across the back of your picture. You can now hang your masterpiece for everyone to enjoy while you get on with the next one.

Sleeping Beauty
Here is a picture that I framed using the method described opposite. I used varnish selectively on this picture, leaving the plaster walls and columns matt.

Fuchsia
I had this picture framed by a professional. She used a deep-rebate frame and wooden fillets to hold the picture away from the glass. She also made more fillets from thin strips of foam-core board covered by mountboard, which she glued to the inside edge of the aperture to form a recessed box.

Index

Suppliers

If you have any difficulty in obtaining any of the items for this craft, please write to the Publishers for an up-to-date list of stockists.

Front cover: ***Cyclamen***
The construction of these cyclamen incorporates over-cutting and careful shaping to make the flowers realistic.

Back cover: ***The apothecary***
This picture incorporates a sloping roof and a foreground with intricate cut-out window frames. The inside of the shop and the courtyard are sub-levels behind the main frontage of the shop.

Strawberries
This print is fairly simple, but attention is needed when cutting the small detailed pieces.